SECRET SHROPSHIRE

The entire proceeds of this book are donated to the Lingen Davies Cancer Fund, The Royal Shrewsbury Hospital, to support quality cancer care for patients in Shropshire and Mid Wales through the funding of specialist equipment and buildings.

SECRET SHROPSHIRE

Copyright © 2013 by Maureen Westerby, Jean Macdonald, Marilyn Gaunt, Helen Jeffery, Melvyn Key, Sally Llewellyn, Moyra Stewart-Wyllie, Helen Bentley, Amy England and Peter Hollingsworth.

The right of the above named to be identified as the authors of this work have been asserted by them in accordance with the Copyright, Designs and Patents Act 1988.

Published by Secret Shropshire Books, 15, Mill Street, Ludlow, Shropshire, SY8 1BE
Project Managed by Patricia Waters, Head of Publishing
Designed and Set by Hannah Perryman and Jacob Geen

First paperback edition in the United Kingdom December 2013
ISBN 978-0-9927740-0-4

Printed and bound in Great Britain by Lightning Source, an Ingram Content Company
www1.lightningsource.com

A catalogue record of this book is available from the British Library.

Copies of this book are available from online retailers.

Front Cover: 'Earth and Trees', Maureen Westerby
Inside Front Cover: 'Wild and Free', The Long Mynd, Jean Macdonald
Opposite Page: Detail from 'The Lineage', Maureen Westerby
Contributing Poets Page: 'The Cherry Tree', Maureen Westerby
Inside Back Cover: 'Forget-me-not', Maureen Westerby
Back Cover: 'Abandoned', Outside Craven Arms, Jean Macdonald

Maureen Westerby - **Artist**

Maureen spent the last part of a rewarding teaching career in Shropshire and only on retirement got the opportunity to follow her dream to become an artist, spending a happy five years studying fine art. With an acute sense of the visual coupled with a home in the heart of the South Shropshire countryside, it was no surprise that recording the landscape would become the central theme of her work. In London Maureen has exhibited work highly commended by The Royal Academy. Exhibitions in Shropshire and Herefordshire have brought her images closer to home.

Jean Macdonald - **Photographer**

Jean's passion for photography took root following careers as a physical training instructor in the Army and later as a physiotherapist. Inspired by the Shropshire landscape on her doorstep, Jean has a natural eye for beauty and an intuitive ability to recognise excellent composition. Her work, published widely, has appeared in Shropshire Life, Amateur Photographer and Farmers Weekly, for whom she has been Photographer of the Year. In 2010 Jean was highly commended in the International Garden Photographer of the Year and Travel Photographer of the Year. In 2012 Jean came first and third in the prestigious International Equine Photographic Competition and has since been highly commended in the British Wildlife Photography Awards 2013. Like Alfred Eisenstaedt, Jean believes, "When I have a camera in my hand, I know no fear."

Marilyn Gaunt - **Principal Poet**

Marilyn studied at Leeds College of Art and The Royal College of Art, Film and T.V. School. She then became a documentary film maker winning a number of awards, including a BAFTA. On retirement Marilyn decided to revisit an earlier passion for poetry. Maureen and Jean's images of their secret Shropshire provided the inspiration and focus she needed to begin writing again.

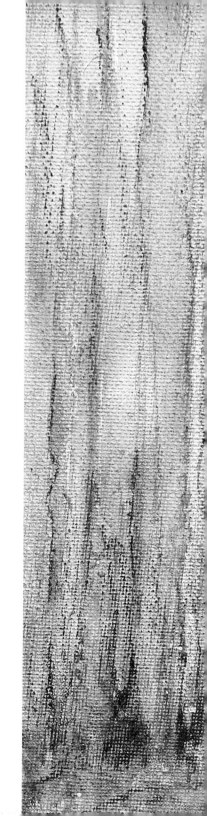

The Wood in February

Under the tangled
underskirts of Clee
we clamber,
my dog Pip and me.
Nets of brambles
tug and snag,
as if to drag us down
to join the Pagan hordes
that fell
upon this ancient ground.

Barren, bracken-broke and bleak,
above the empty trees
the air is still.
The only sound
the drip of water on dead leaves.
Their grave a womb,
the silence
pregnant
with the hope
of Spring.

Marilyn Gaunt

Dawn

A shaft of sunlight through the trees,
a glimpse of something brighter at the end of the tunnel.
From the first faint trace of not quite darkness dawn,
light banishes the demons,
leads us on.

Helen Jeffery

Ice Age

Fractured rocks,
ice broke.
And ghosts of trees that once,
with fragile hope,
grew.
In spite of glacial currents
that solid rock could hew,
and wear and roll
into pebbled jewels.
The birches quivered,
clinging on to life
under a watery
sun.

Marilyn Gaunt

The Covering

Dew caresses the countryside,
Revealing silken eyes,
Wide-open.

Mel Key

Nature's Army

Green regiments
Spring to attention
From April earth.
Ready for battle
Against
Late frost,
Flood, slug and dearth
Of rain.

Their victory
Ripe
Full-grown
Full-blown
Summer.

Marilyn Gaunt

Poppies

Vermilion cups of pleated silk
set the pasture ablaze.

Sally Llewellyn

Remembrance

What unknown countryman
lies beneath
to turn my petals red?
What ploughman, weaver, tailor, thief
helps make our Nation's bread?
This corn that grows in peace and warmth
under a Shropshire sky
gives life to those who followed on,
to those who did not die.

Marilyn Gaunt

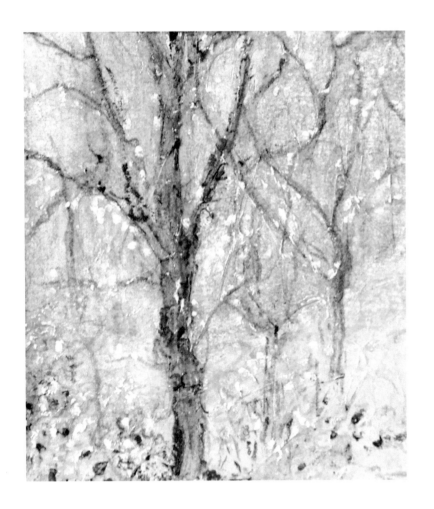

Woods in Sunshine

In shafts of
sunlight
through the trees
I pass
fractured light
against a sky of
virgin blue
splinters gold
across the bluebell's bank.

No work of Man
can out-surpass
with columns of stone
and manufactured glass
the beauty Nature
squanders
on the grass.

Marilyn Gaunt

Misty Morning

Soft
pastel
shades
the
shifting
shapes
of
sunlight
on
twig
and
branch
and
bough.

Sally Llewellyn

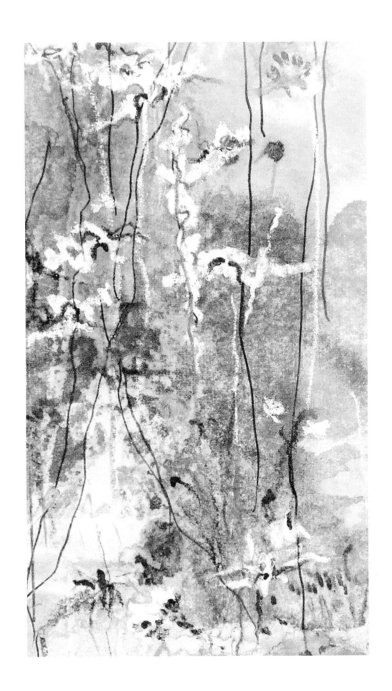

In Praise of Those
Who Saved the Kite

To protect those golden foreigners
Brought here to breed and kill
The kite became a stranger
Hardly seen on Shropshire hill

For pheasant need protection
From predators like me
So they can reach adulthood
And give the marksman glee

So full of hate with poisoned bait
The gamekeepers began
The cull of buzzard,kite and crow
To help the sport of Man

And yet, among the thermals,
I hang and hover still
A symbol of survival
And of other men's Goodwill

Marilyn Gaunt

Out of Touch

Is the last putting of pieces together
to be alone, to hear soft-stepping
deer in the woods, the leaves exhale
in the night, fox calling and the hopeful
chirp of new-hatched bird. To be,
undisturbed, watching the short light
lengthen, flash in the dew-drained web.
To go home - the well of remembrance
spilled over - walking on the web of roots
the mesh of veins re-iterate, touching.

Moyra Stewart-Wyllie

Nature in Limbo

Purple mist
hails the dawn,
creeps from deep
within the trees.
Foxgloves sway
unaware of what is
coming in the breeze.

Brief moments
captured
with a quiet
observer's lens,
nature in limbo
waits as night
to morning bends.

Helen Bentley

Daybreak

Mist and mystery
Hover under ancient trees.
As, in the depths,
Life shifts and breathes
Its warmth up
To the morning's
Chill.

Marilyn Gaunt

Morning Glory

The morning light shines down in the forest glen
the linear warmth waking the new day
branches come to life enchanted
waving within the weighty wind.

Amy England

Heatwave's End

After cauldron days of glorious sun
The weather's turn approaches.
The breathless, heavy air,
Sucked out by suffocating heat
Is still.
Thick with anticipation,
Thunderheads climb the horizon.
The storm's first warning growl
Sends bees to hive
And sheep to sheltering trees.

And I lie down
Back braced against the sun-parched grass
Preparing for the thunder's deafening roar
The lightning's flash.
Mouth open to drink in, like earth,
The sky's life-giving blood.
The flood and sound as old
As Earth's creation.

Marilyn Gaunt

Far Horizons

Islands in a mist
That softly settles,
A world silenced by whiteness
Far horizons cloaked by cloud,
Turn Shropshire
Into Shangri-La.

Here Galahad can seek The Grail
And Arthur's funeral ship can sail
Across to distant Avalon.
And Kubla Khan can build again
Upon this hidden Marches plain
Pavilions splendid to the view,
In a wondrous
Shropshire Xanadu.

Marilyn Gaunt

The Lonely Tree

I stand a lone survivor
Of hedges seven miles long,
Of copse and tangled forest
Full of fox and bright birdsong.
Thanks to a kindly farmer,
Who perhaps enjoyed my grace,
I came in last position
In extinction's nasty race.
Now, as the combine harvester
Steers round my spreading crown
And creaks across my tired old roots
I'm glad I'm not cut down.
For birds still gather in my hair
And sing me tales of places where
A million trees still spread and reach
The Willow, Pine and lofty Beech,
In joyful, dense communication;
The last surviving woodland nation.
And I recall the tribe I've lost,
And contemplate survival's cost.

Marilyn Gaunt

Woodland Haze

Within the wood I wander
Within a dream I seem
From tree to tree I stumble
Nature's hold falls over me

Amy England

In Company of Trees

In the wilderness of winter, when nature's gone to ground
Lowlands are flooded, sunlight filters down
I'll wander in the byways, once again to see
The tracery and form of winter's trees.

Through changing seasons, ease is given me
In company of trees.

In the wakening that follows winter's weary night
When everything's responsive to the catalyst of light
I'll wander in the country, once again to see
The fresh unfolding foliage of trees.

Through changing seasons, ease is given me
In company of trees.

In the drowsiness of summer, when watercourses dry
And cattle seek for shelter from an overbearing sky
I'll follow forest footpaths, once again to be
Beneath the canopy of trees.

Through changing seasons, ease is given me
In company of trees.

In 'mists and mellow fruitfulness', the earth we hold dear
Has yielded up her harvest: the crowning of the year.
I'll walk among the woodlands, once again to see
The pageantry and colours of trees.

Through changing seasons
Ease comes to me
In company of trees
In the glory and gracefulness of trees.

Peter Hollingsworth

Woodland Ways

Some folk think woods are wonderful,
They love the smell of mould
And trunks of trees like prison bars
To them seem wise and old.
They love the crunch of foot on leaf,
They love the sudden rush
Of wild things startled as they pass,
They love the moss-hung hush.
The hoot of owl and fox's howl
Are music to their ears,
But all these things for me disturb
Primeval thoughts and fears.
Oh, give to me the upland ways,
With hills and vistas wide,
The meadows and the windswept moors,
Where things that kill can't hide!

Marilyn Gaunt

A Tree

A tree is a trunk,
is a branch, is a leaf,
a place of relief
for an oxygen thief.

Amy England

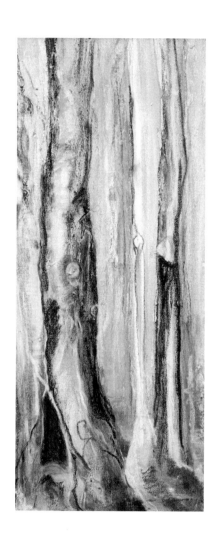

Birches

In a moonlight,
delicate and glimmering,
the trees glow ghostly white.
By night,
the haunt of silent swooping owls.
By day,
a hide for butterflies,
fluttering through the lace
of their bright green hair.

Marilyn Gaunt

The Eternal Song

Colours dance in dangled branch
they waltz to nature's song,
cut it, saw it, chop it down
but the waltz goes on and on.

Amy England

Into The Woods

There's light at the end of the tunnel
My granny always said
As I skip along the moonlit path
Red hood pulled round my head
I will keep to the bright
And well trod road
That beckons up ahead
For I dare not stray along the way
Into the woods I dread
Remembering blood soaked axes
Of the sort woodcutters wield
I begin to wish that Granny's house
Was in an open field.

Marilyn Gaunt

Light's Muse

An earthen warmth spreads
Around each of nature's columns,
A shaft of light, a tree's delight
At shapely shadows fallen.

Amy England

Ludlow

Looking over Ludlow at the rising of the sun
From the hill above the river where the silver salmon run
A rosebud unfolding, its petals soon undone
In beauty and innocence the day has just begun

Looking down on Ludlow from the high church tower
As the clock chimes and counts down the noontide hour
In the market, the cheery, the deft, and the dour
The caring, the cursing, the sweet and the sour

Looking beyond Ludlow from the ancient castle wall
To Clee hill and to Clun as the evening shadows fall
Commerce is quieted, distant curlews call
Forgive us our trespasses, forgive us, all

Peter Hollingsworth

Wild Ponies of The Mynd

Along the ridges
of these ancient hills,
Ancestral Sires,
backs gripped by thighs
of Caradoc's kind,
carried them to victory and defeat.
No longer free,
our Grand Mares
dragged into the Underworld.
The dark and heat
of coal black pits.
Banished from bracken,
curlew's call and skylark skies.
Released at last,
returning to the light.
Promethean ponies
answered the call of the wild,
the cry of kites.
Surviving blizzards,
hail and quiet moonlit nights,
along the ridges of this
Shropshire hill,
we forage still.

Marilyn Gaunt

Winter

Shards of pale light
Crystals of frozen water cloak the trees
Winter's breath

Mel Key

INDEX OF IMAGES

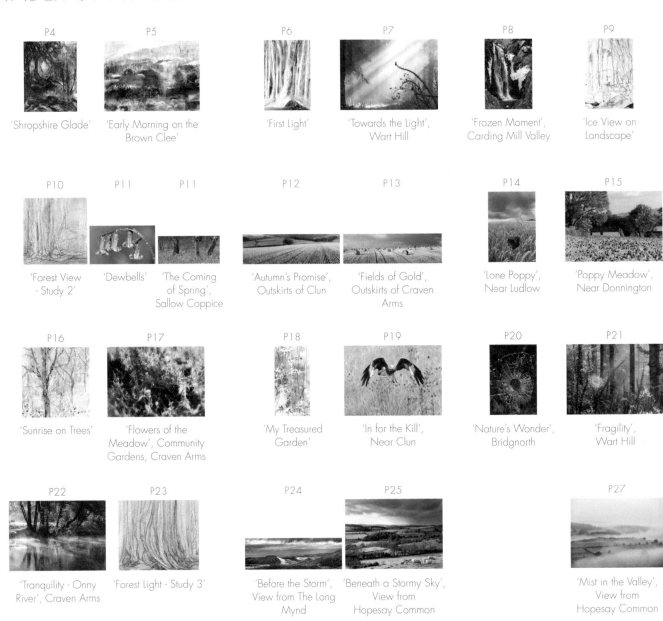

P28
'Lone Tree',
View from Lawley Hill

P29
'Survival'

P30
'Between Earth and Sky', View from Nordy Bank

P31
'Call of the Wild', The Long Mynd

P32
'Woodland Spirit'

P33
'River Scene, Bridgnorth'

P35
'Evening Light', View from Hopesay Common

P36
'Knarled Woodland'

P37
'In the Spotlight', View from Hopesay Common

P38
'Autumn Glory'

P39
'Moonlight'

P39
'Standing Tall', Apley Wood

P40
'Tree on Blue'

P41
'A Carpet of Gold', Mortimer Forest

P42
'Walk on the Brown Clee'

P43
'The Secret Path', Wart Hill

P44
'Earth and Trees'

P45
'Enchanted Forest', Near Craven Arms

P46
'Morning Glory', Ludlow

P47
'Stormy Castle', Clun

P48
'Surviving the Blizzard', The Long Mynd

P49
'Winter Feed', The Long Mynd

P50
'Ice Patterns', The Long Mynd

P51
'Hoar Frost Trees', The Long Mynd

Artwork by **Maureen Westerby**   Photography by **Jean Macdonald** – www.behindmylens.co.uk

Project Managed by Patricia Waters, Head of Publishing.

Designed and set by Hannah Perryman and Jacob Geen.

CONTRIBUTING POETS:

Helen Jeffery, born in South Wales, studied ecology and genetics at York University. Along with her two lovely daughters, environmental concerns have been her priority. Her work has always involved young people with twelve caring years spent teaching in Shropshire.

Mel Key, born and bred in England now lives with his wife Linda in a small village north of Toronto, in what is referred to as cottage country. Mel is a retired teacher. His interest in haiku was kindled by his youngest son's Japanese partner, Hiroko.

Sally Llewellyn has had a lifelong love of art and the Shropshire countryside. Now retired, she has more time for painting, drawing and writing, focusing mainly on animals and the landscape. Her interest in the past has led her to read Humanities with Classical Studies.

Moyra Stewart-Wyllie began writing poetry as a child growing up in mid-Wales. She has lived in Shropshire for the past twenty years and takes her inspiration from a sense of place, history and the landscape.

Helen Bentley married husband Tim in Shropshire and they live now in Indiana, U.S.A. with their children Matt and Issy. She has an M.A. in English and teaches English at Ivy Tech in Lafayette. Helen also performs and writes for the musical duo of which she is a part.

Amy England has been creative all her life. Ten years ago she moved to Shropshire and fell in love with the beauty and serenity of the countryside. This is now the inspiration for her work.

Peter Hollingsworth, an engineer/teacher has always loved 'wandering by lone sea-breakers, and sitting by desolate streams' (O'Shaughnessy). He rejoices in the breath-taking beauty of Border County countryside and feels compelled to share this in poetry.

Maureen, Jean and Marilyn would like to thank their families and friends for their invaluable love and support.

THIS BOOK IS DEDICATED TO:

Eileen Bentley and Patricia Waters for the conception of the idea, their hard work, enthusiasm and the belief that it was possible.

The staff and students of Lower Bush Farm Rural Skills Centre for their constant support.

The Discovery Centre, Craven Arms for hosting the exhibition Secret Shropshire.

Dr Agrawal and the oncology team at the Lingen Davies Centre, The Royal Shrewsbury Hospital, Shropshire.

Forget-me-not

There, by the starlit fences,
The wanderer halts and hears
My soul that lingers sighing
About the glimmering weirs.

Excerpt taken from 'Far in a Western
Brookland', from 'A Shropshire Lad'
(1896) by A.E. Housman (1859-1936).

Lightning Source UK Ltd.
Milton Keynes UK
UKIC01n0645111213
222784UK00002B/16

9 780099 274004